Alfred's Basic Piano I

Piano

Ear Training Book
Level 3

Gayle Kowalchyk • E. L. Lancaster

Alfred Music
P.O. Box 10003
Van Nuys, CA 91410-0003
alfred.com

ISBN-10: 0-7390-0598-7
ISBN-13: 978-0-7390-0598-9

Cover Illustration by David Silverman

Instructions for Use

1. This EAR TRAINING BOOK is designed to be used with Alfred's Basic Piano Library, LESSON BOOK 3.

2. This book is coordinated page-by-page with the LESSON BOOK, and assignments are ideally made according to the instructions in the upper right corner of each page of the EAR TRAINING BOOK.

3. Many students enjoy completing these pages so much that they will want to go beyond the assigned material. However, it is best to wait until the indicated pages in the LESSON BOOK have been covered before the corresponding material in this book is studied.

4. This EAR TRAINING BOOK reinforces each concept presented in the LESSON BOOK and specifically focuses on the training and development of the ear. Rhythmic, melodic and intervallic concepts are drilled throughout the book to provide the necessary systematic reinforcement for the student.

5. Each page is designed to be completed using approximately five minutes of the lesson time. Examples for each page are given for the teacher (pages 38–48).

Review

1. Your teacher will play a melody in $\frac{3}{4}$ or $\frac{4}{4}$ time.
   - Circle $\frac{3}{4}$ if you hear 3 beats in each measure.
   - Circle $\frac{4}{4}$ if you hear 4 beats in each measure.

2. Your teacher will play a bass pattern. Circle the pattern that you hear.

3. Your teacher will play a melody.
   Add the appropriate dynamic marking (*mf* or *p*) on the lines below the staff.

4. Your teacher will clap a rhythm pattern. Circle the pattern that you hear.

5. Your teacher will play an interval of a 5th or 6th. Circle the interval that you hear.

1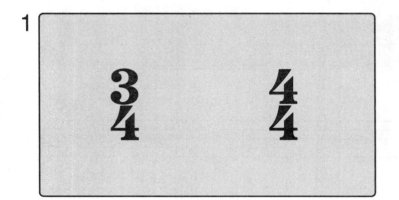

2

3

4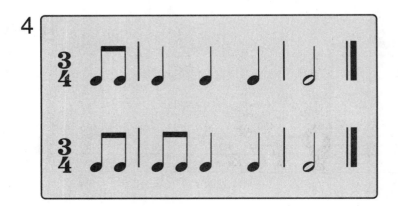

5

TEACHER: See page 38.

4

Review

1. Your teacher will play a melody.

   • Add a CRESCENDO sign (<) UNDER the staff if the melody gets GRADUALLY LOUDER.

   • Add a DIMENUENDO sign (>) UNDER the staff if the melody gets GRADUALLY SOFTER.

2. Your teacher will play a melody that contains a RITARDANDO. Add the RITARDANDO (*rit.*) below the staff when the tempo begins to GRADUALLY SLOW DOWN.

3. Your teacher will play a MELODIC interval of a 2nd or 3rd ABOVE the given note.
   • Draw the second note on the staff using a half note.
   • Write the interval number (2 or 3) on the line.

4. Your teacher will clap a rhythm pattern.
   Draw the missing notes in the third measure, using ♩ and ♫

5. Your teacher will play a melody that uses six notes (C-D-E-F-G-A).
   Draw the missing notes in the third measure, using the correct rhythm.

An Extended Position

1. Your teacher will play four melodies, some of which use an EXTENDED POSITION.
   Circle the melody that you hear.

2. Your teacher will play a BLOCK chord followed by a BROKEN chord.
   Write the notes of the BROKEN chord in the order that they are played, using QUARTER notes.

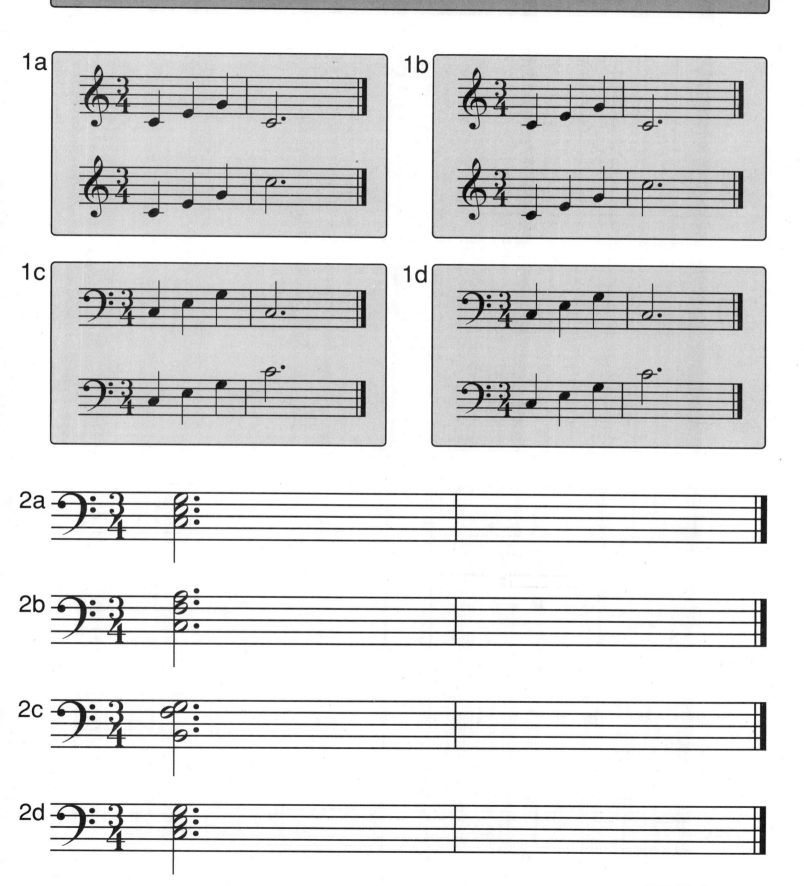

6

Extended Positions in G and D Major

1. Your teacher will play four melodies, some of which use EXTENDED POSITIONS, in G and D major. Circle the melody that you hear.
2. Your teacher will play **I**, **IV** and **V⁷** chords in the keys of G and D major. Circle the chords that you hear.

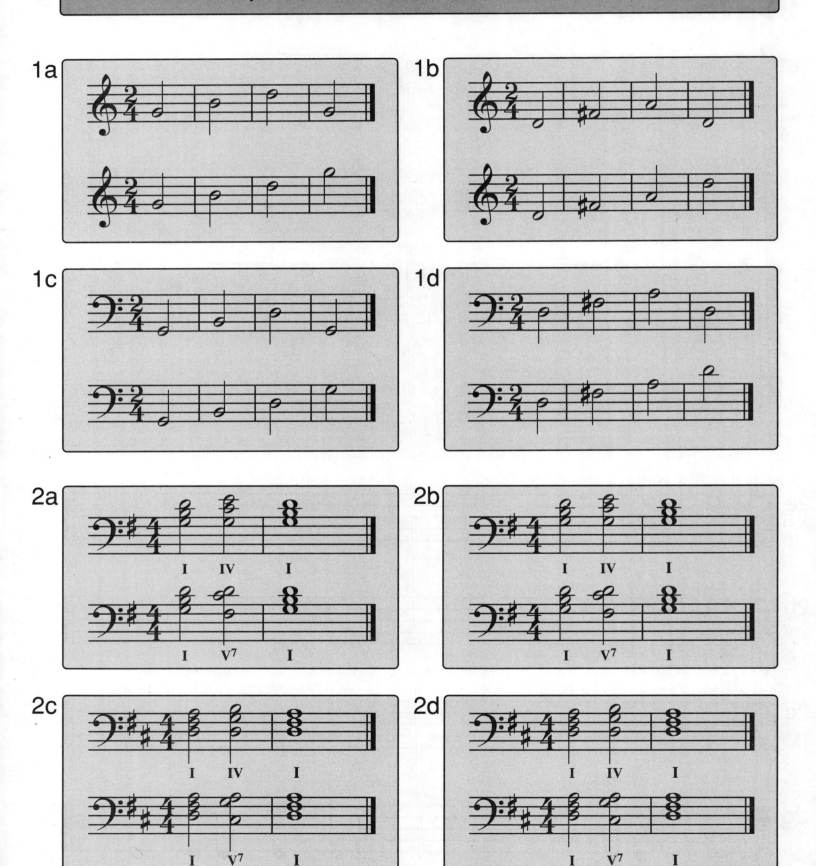

Primary Chords

1. Your teacher will play groups of PRIMARY CHORDS. Each group contains a RITARDANDO.
   Add the RITARDANDO (*rit.*) below the staff when the tempo begins to GRADUALLY SLOW DOWN.
2. Your teacher will clap a rhythm pattern.
   Draw the missing notes in the second measure, using ♩ ♩ or ♫

Use with pages 8–9.

Primary Chords

1. Your teacher will play **I**, **IV** and **V⁷** chords in the keys of C, G and D major.
   Write the Roman numeral name for the missing chords on the lines.
2. Your teacher will play melodies and chords in C, G and D major.
   Write the Roman numeral names (**I**, **IV** or **V⁷**) on the lines below the staff.

1a   **I**   **V⁷**   _____   _____

1b   **IV**   _____   **V⁷**   _____

1c   **V⁷**   **I**   _____   _____

1d   **I**   _____   _____   **I**

2a   **I**

2b   **IV**

2c   **I**

Accompaniment Patterns

1. Your teacher will play a left hand accompaniment pattern.
   Circle the pattern that you hear.

2. Your teacher will play MELODIC intervals of a 4th, 5th or 6th ABOVE the given note.
   • Draw the second note on the staff, using a half note.
   • Write the interval name (4, 5 or 6) on the line.

1a

1b

1c
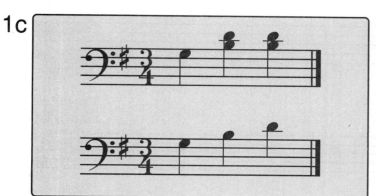

1d

2a

2b

2c
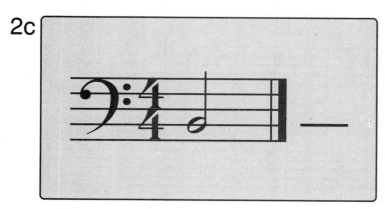

2d
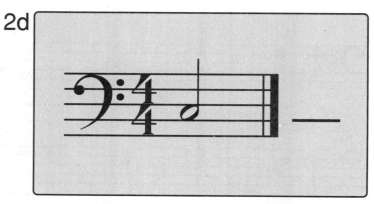

TEACHER: See page 39.

Use with pages 12–13.

8va

1. Your teacher will play four melodies. Add an 8va sign (*8va - - - - - - ¬*) above the notes that are played one octave HIGHER than written.
2. Your teacher will play four accompaniment patterns. Each pattern contains one ACCENT. Add an ACCENT SIGN under (♩) or over (♪) the note(s) that are played LOUDER.
                       >   >

Accompaniment Patterns

1. Your teacher will play a left hand accompaniment pattern.
   Circle the pattern that you hear.

2. Your teacher will play four melodies. Two notes in each melody will be played incorrectly.
   Circle the incorrect notes.

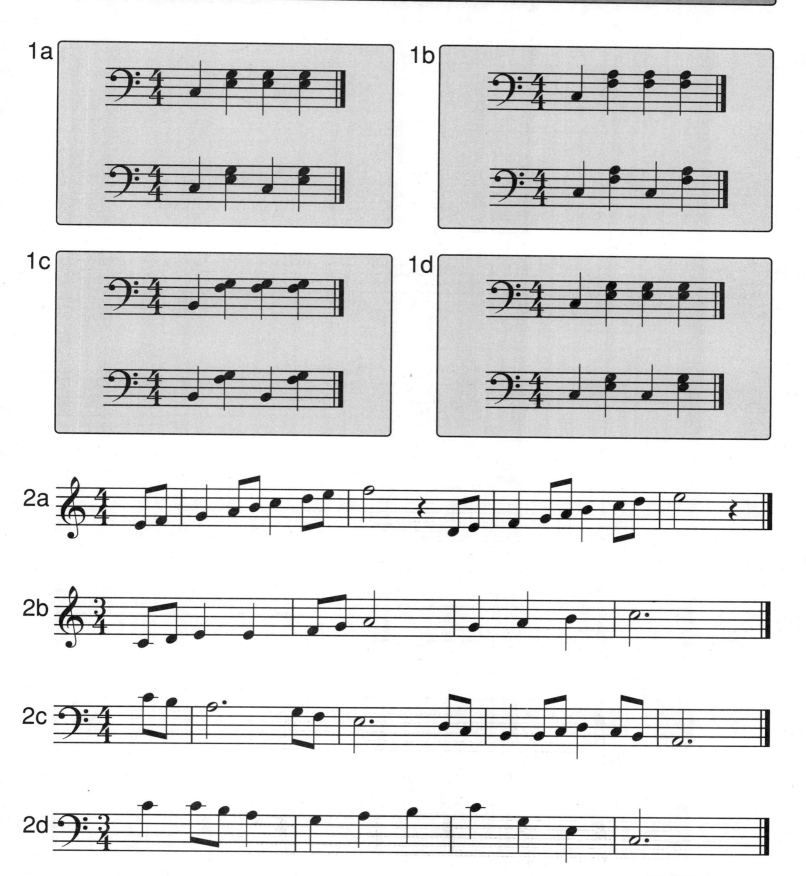

1a 1b 1c 1d

2a 2b 2c 2d

TEACHER: See page 40.

Use with pages 16–17.

Major Scales

1. Your teacher will play MAJOR SCALES that move in the SAME direction or in CONTRARY MOTION. Circle SAME if the scales move in the SAME direction. Circle CONTRARY if the scales move in CONTRARY MOTION.

2. Your teacher will play melodies that use notes from the C, G and D MAJOR SCALES. Draw the missing notes in the second measure, using the correct rhythm.

1a

SAME

CONTRARY

1b

SAME

CONTRARY

1c

SAME

CONTRARY

1d

SAME

CONTRARY

The Chromatic Scale

1. Your teacher will play a MAJOR or CHROMATIC scale.
   Circle MAJOR if you hear a MAJOR scale. Circle CHROMATIC if you hear a CHROMATIC scale.
2. Your teacher will play four melodies.
   Circle the melody that you hear.

1a

MAJOR

CHROMATIC

1b

MAJOR

CHROMATIC

1c

MAJOR

CHROMATIC

1d

MAJOR

CHROMATIC

2a

2b

2c

2d

TEACHER: See page 41.

14

Use with page 19.

The Chromatic Scale

1. Your teacher will play melodies that use CHROMATIC SCALE patterns. Draw the missing notes in the third measure, using the correct rhythm. Use SHARPS to indicate BLACK KEYS in ASCENDING patterns. Use FLATS to indicate BLACK KEYS in DESCENDING patterns.

2. Your teacher will play a left hand accompaniment pattern.
   Circle the pattern that you hear.

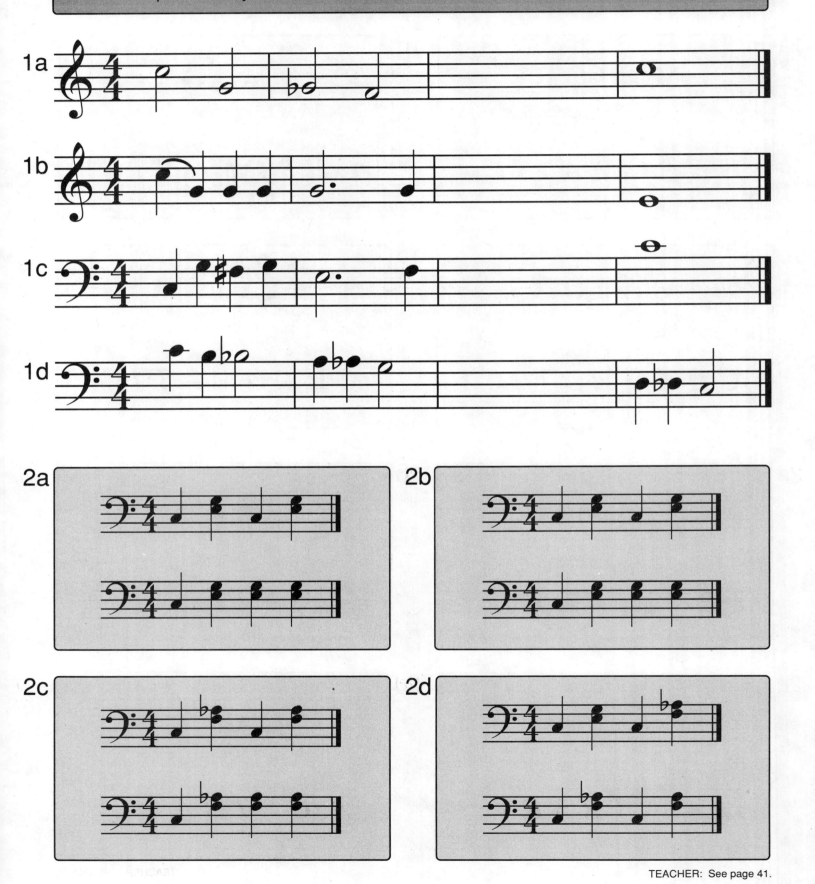

TEACHER: See page 41.

The F Major Scale

1. Your teacher will play F MAJOR SCALES. One note in each scale will be played incorrectly. Circle the incorrect note.
2. Your teacher will play F MAJOR SCALES that move in the SAME direction or in CONTRARY MOTION. Circle SAME if the scales move in the SAME direction. Circle CONTRARY if the scales move in CONTRARY MOTION.

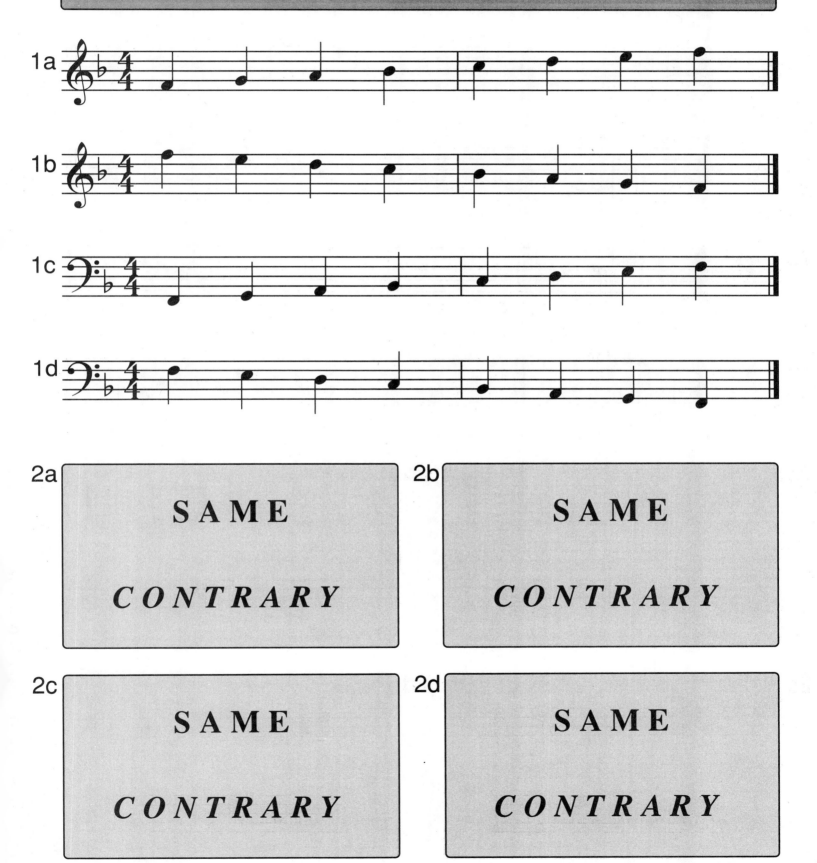

Use with page 21.

The F Major Scale

1. Your teacher will play melodies that use notes from the F MAJOR SCALE.
   Draw the missing notes in the second measure, using the correct rhythm.

2. Your teacher will play F MAJOR SCALES.
   Circle the rhythm pattern that you hear for each scale.

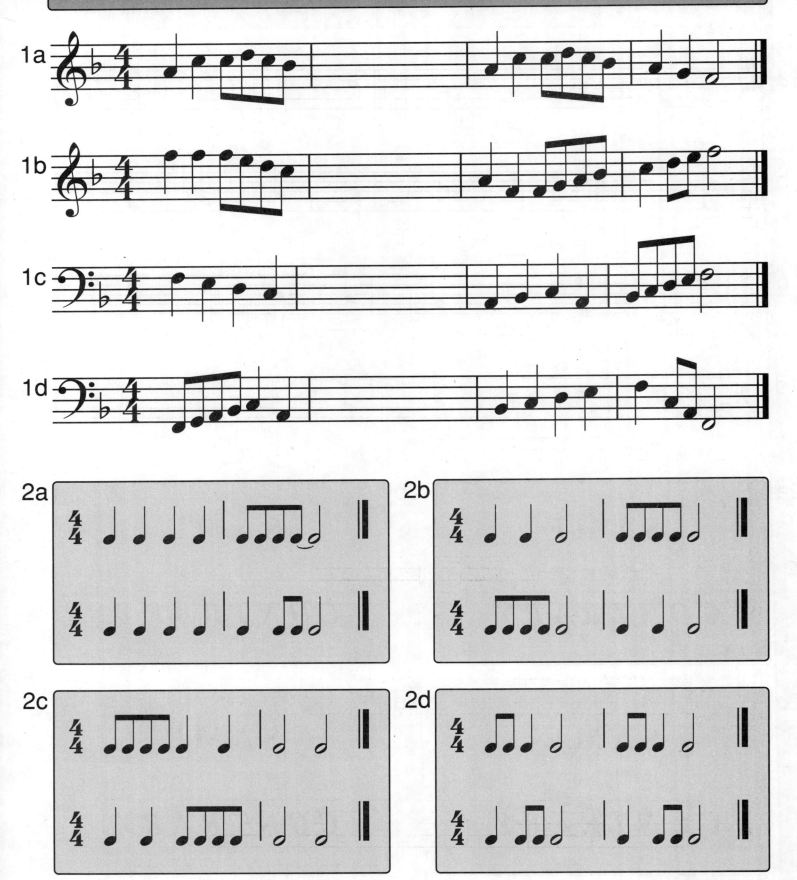

TEACHER: See page 42.

Primary Chords in F Major

1. Your teacher will play **I**, **IV** and **V⁷** chords in the key of F.
   Write the Roman numeral name for each chord on the line. The first chord is shown.
2. Your teacher will clap a rhythm pattern.
   Draw the missing notes in the second measure, using  or

1a $\underline{\quad I \quad}$ $\underline{\qquad}$ $\underline{\qquad}$ $\underline{\qquad}$

1b $\underline{\quad I \quad}$ $\underline{\qquad}$ $\underline{\qquad}$ $\underline{\qquad}$

1c $\underline{\quad V7 \quad}$ $\underline{\qquad}$ $\underline{\qquad}$ $\underline{\qquad}$

1d $\underline{\quad IV \quad}$ $\underline{\qquad}$ $\underline{\qquad}$ $\underline{\qquad}$

2a

2b

2c

2d

TEACHER: See page 42.

Use with pages 22–23.

Primary Chords in F Major

1. Your teacher will play a BLOCK chord followed by a BROKEN chord.
   Write the notes of the BROKEN chord in the order that they are played, using QUARTER notes.
2. Your teacher will play melodies, some of which use an EXTENDED POSITION.
   Circle the melody that you hear.

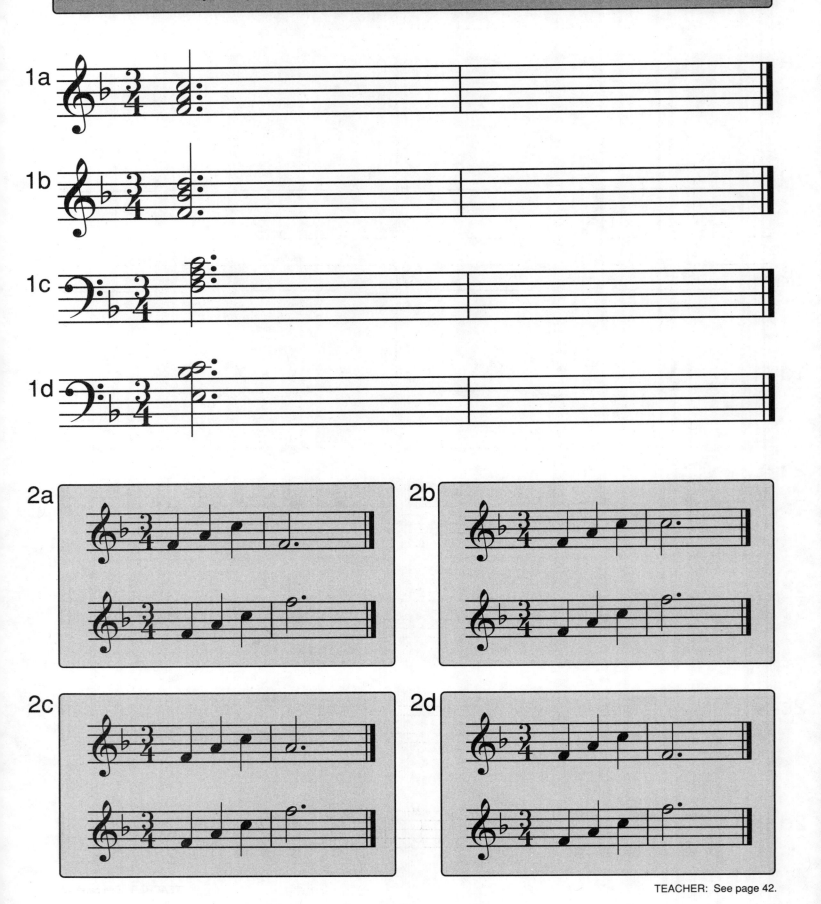

TEACHER: See page 42.

Minor Scales

1. Your teacher will play a MAJOR SCALE or a NATURAL MINOR SCALE.
   Circle MAJOR if you hear a MAJOR SCALE. Circle MINOR if you hear a MINOR SCALE.
2. Your teacher will play the A NATURAL MINOR SCALE or the A MELODIC MINOR SCALE.
   If the scale is MELODIC MINOR, draw a SHARP (♯) in front of the 6th and 7th tones in the
   ASCENDING SCALE.

TEACHER: See page 42.

Use with page 25.

Harmonic Minor Scales

1. Your teacher will play the A NATURAL MINOR SCALE or the A HARMONIC MINOR SCALE. If the scale is HARMONIC MINOR, draw a SHARP (♯) in front of the 7th tones.

2. Your teacher will play intervals of a 6th, 7th or 8th (octave) ABOVE the given note from the A HARMONIC MINOR SCALE.
   • Draw the second note on the staff, using a half note.
   • Write the interval name (6, 7 or 8) on the line.

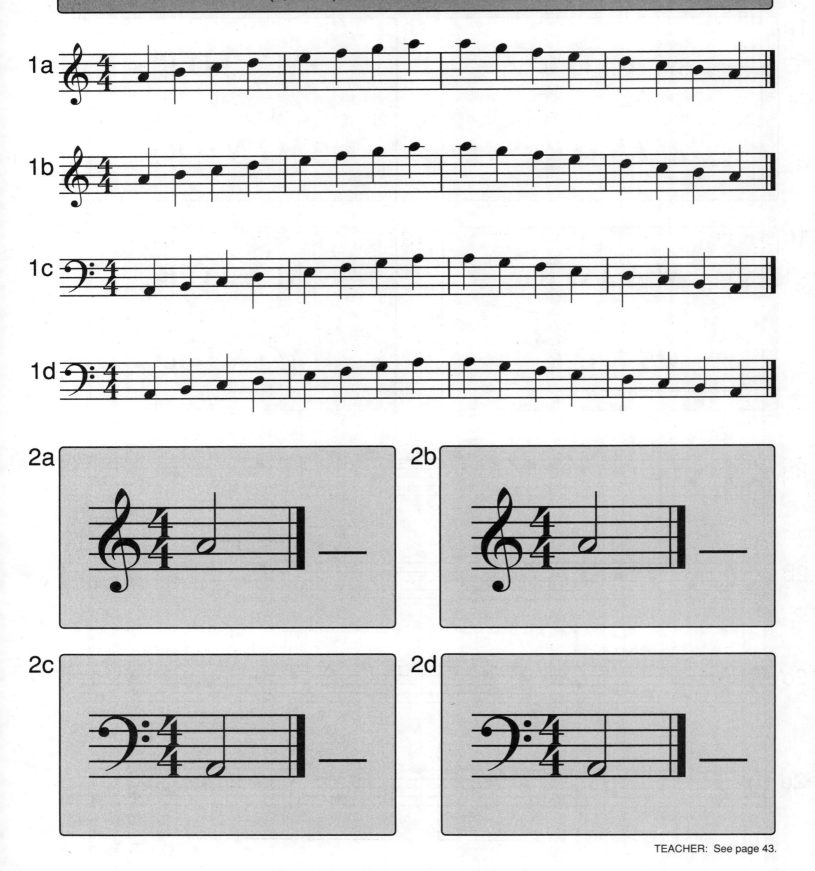

TEACHER: See page 43.

3rds and 5ths

1. Your teacher will play a MAJOR 3rd or a MINOR 3rd.
   Circle MAJOR if you hear a MAJOR 3rd. Circle MINOR if you hear a MINOR 3rd.

2. Your teacher will play intervals of a MAJOR 3rd or a PERFECT 5th ABOVE the given note.
   • Draw the second note on the staff, using a half note.
   • Write the interval name (M3 or P5) on the line.

1a

MAJOR

MINOR

1b

MAJOR

MINOR

1c

MAJOR

MINOR

1d

MAJOR

MINOR

2a

2b

2c
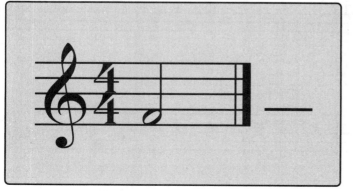

2d
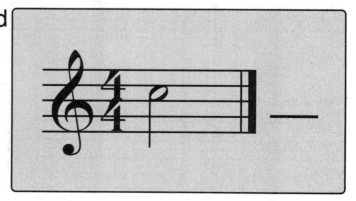

TEACHER: See page 43.

22

Use with page 27.

Major and Minor

1. Your teacher will play a MAJOR or MINOR melody. Write MAJOR in the blank if the melody is in a MAJOR KEY. Write MINOR in the blank if the melody is in a MINOR KEY.
2. Your teacher will play four melodies.
   Add the appropriate dynamic marking (*mf* or *p*) on the lines below the staff.

1a _____

1b _____

1c _____

1d _____

2a

2b

2c

2d

TEACHER: See page 43.

Major and Minor Triads

1. Your teacher will play a MAJOR or MINOR triad.
   Circle the triad that you hear.

2. Your teacher will play four melodies. Two notes in each melody will be played incorrectly.
   Circle the incorrect notes.

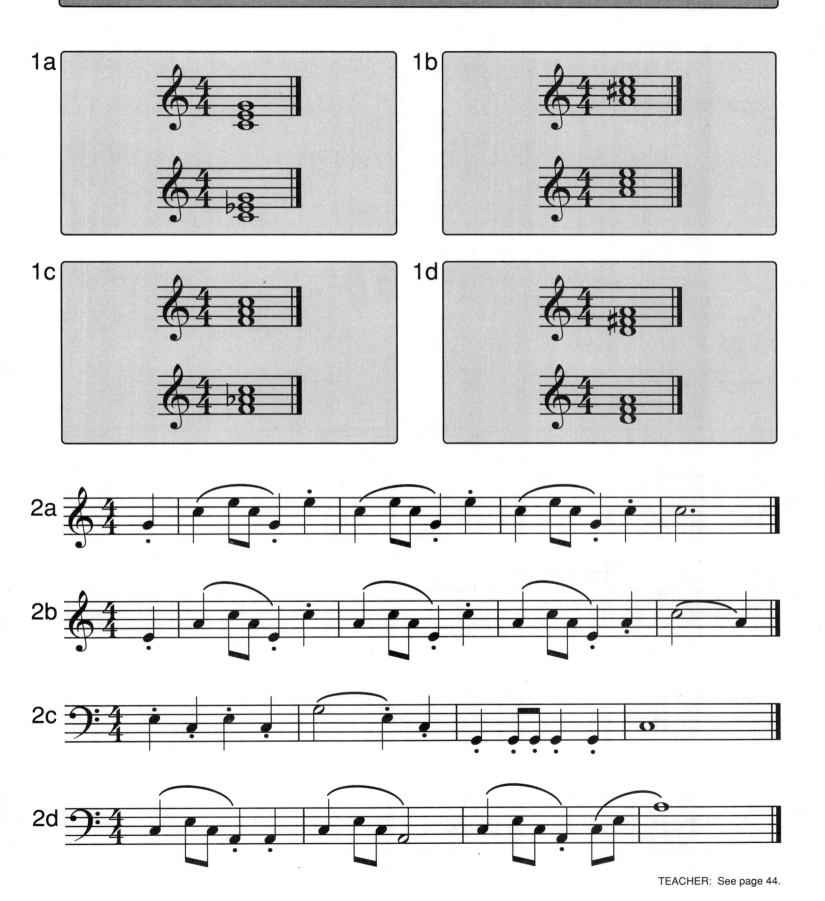

24

Use with pages 28–29.

Major and Minor Triads

1. Your teacher will play MAJOR and MINOR triads.
   Write M for each MAJOR triad and m for each MINOR TRIAD.

2. Your teacher will play a BLOCK chord followed by a BROKEN chord.
   Write the notes of the BROKEN chord in the order that they are played, using QUARTER notes.

1a _____   1e _____

1b _____   1f _____

1c _____   1g _____

1d _____   1h _____

2a

2b

2c

2d

Pedal

1. Your teacher will play four melodies. Draw a PEDAL SIGN ( ) under the entire melody if the DAMPER PEDAL is used.
2. Your teacher will clap a rhythm pattern. Draw the missing notes in the third measure, using ♩ ♫ ♩ ♩ ♩. or ♪

Use with pages 32–33.

Melody and Accompaniment

1. Your teacher will play melodies that use notes from the A HARMONIC MINOR SCALE.
   Draw the missing notes in the third measure, using the correct rhythm.

2. Your teacher will play a left hand accompaniment pattern.
   Circle the pattern that you hear.

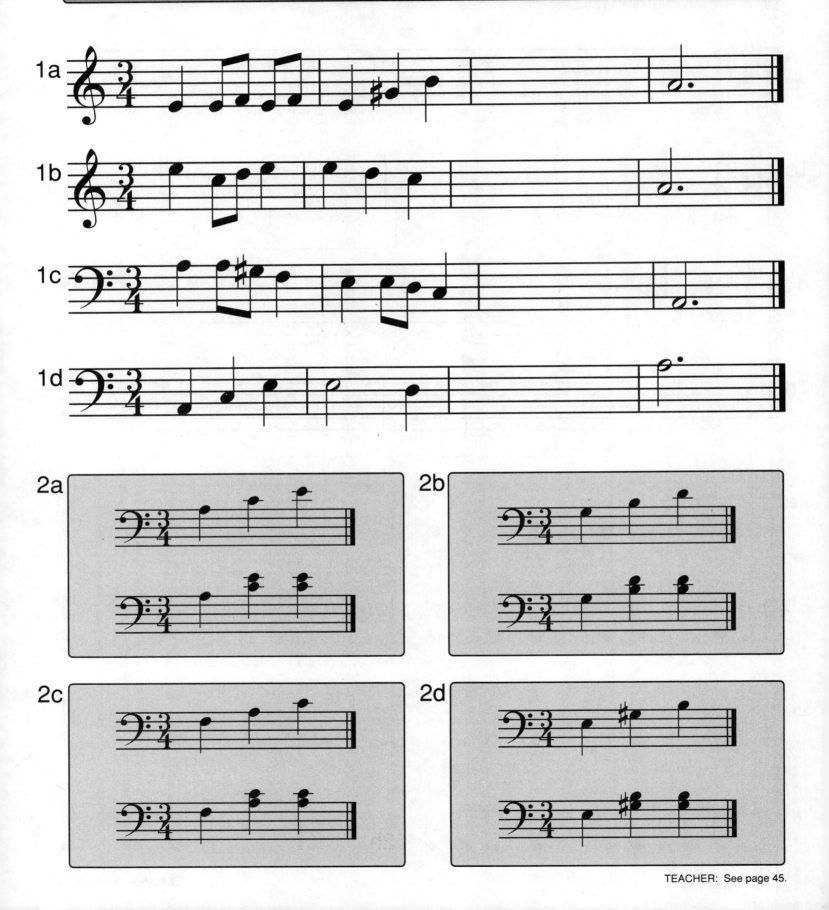

Primary Triads in Minor Keys

1. Your teacher will play A minor chord progressions.
    Circle the progression that you hear.
2. Your teacher will play **i**, **iv** and **V** chords in the key of A minor.
    Write the Roman numeral name for the missing chord on the line.

1a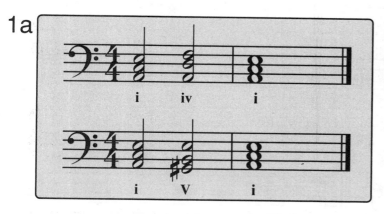

1b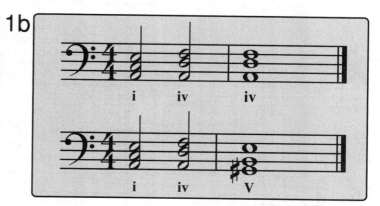

1c

1d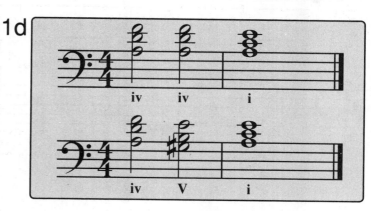

2a **i** _____ **i**

2b **i** _____ **iv**

2c **i** _____ **V**

2d **i** _____ **V**

2e **i** _____ **i**

2f **i** _____ **V**

2g **i** _____ **iv**

2h **i** _____ **i**

28

Primary Triads in A Minor

1. Your teacher will play melodies and chords in A minor.
   Write the Roman numeral names (**i**, **iv** or **V**) on the lines below the staff.

2. Your teacher will play four melodies.
   • Add a CRESCENDO sign (————————) UNDER the staff if the melody gets
   GRADUALLY LOUDER.
   • Add a DIMINUENDO sign (————————) UNDER the staff if the melody gets
   GRADUALLY SOFTER.

TEACHER: See page 45.

Primary Chords in A Minor

1. Your teacher will play **i**, **iv** and **V⁷** chords in the key of A minor.
   Write the Roman numeral name for each chord. The first chord is shown.

2. Your teacher will play a chord progression.
   Circle the progression that you hear.

1a   <u> **i** </u>   _____   _____   _____

1b   <u> **i** </u>   _____   _____   _____

1c   <u> **iv** </u>   _____   _____   _____

1d   <u> **iv** </u>   _____   _____   _____

2a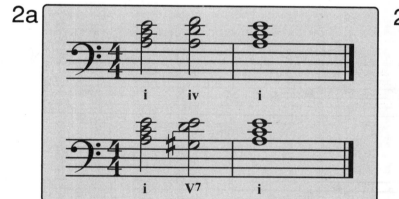

2b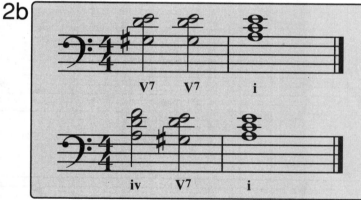

2c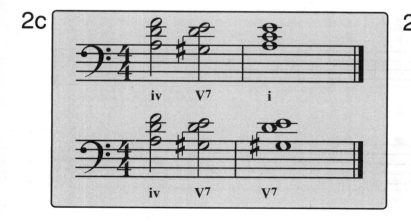

2d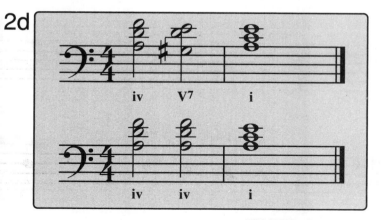

TEACHER: See page 46.

Use with page 38.

The Key of D Minor

1. Your teacher will play the D NATURAL MINOR SCALE or the D HARMONIC MINOR SCALE.
   If the scale is HARMONIC MINOR, draw a SHARP (♯) in front of the 7th tones.

2. Your teacher will play the D NATURAL MINOR SCALE or the D MELODIC MINOR SCALE.
   If the scale is MELODIC MINOR, raise the 6th and 7th tones one half step (to B & C♯)
   in the ASCENDING SCALE.

The Key of D Minor

1. Your teacher will play a left hand accompaniment pattern. Circle the pattern that you hear.
2. Your teacher will play intervals of a 6th, 7th or 8th (octave) ABOVE the given note from the D HARMONIC MINOR SCALE.
   • Draw the second note on the staff, using a half note.
   • Write the interval name (6, 7 or 8) on the line.

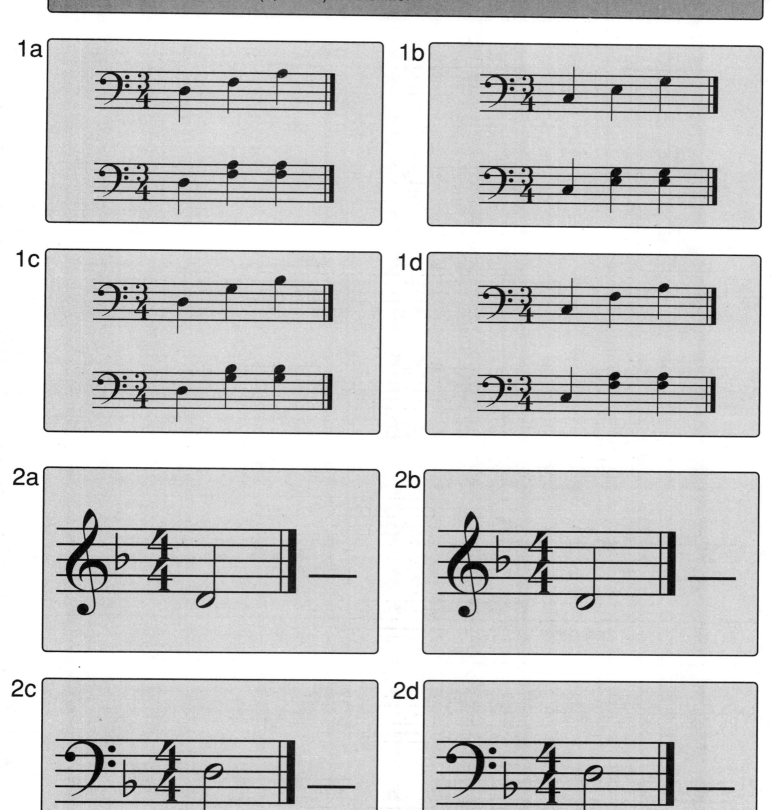

Use with pages 40–41.

Primary Chords in D Minor

1. Your teacher will play **i**, **iv** and **V⁷** chords in the key of D minor.
   Write the Roman numeral name for each chord. The first chord is shown.

2. Your teacher will play a chord progression.
   Circle the progression that you hear.

1a   ___**i**___   _____   _____   _____

1b   ___**iv**___   _____   _____   _____

1c   ___**iv**___   _____   _____   _____

1d   ___**i**___   _____   _____   _____

2a
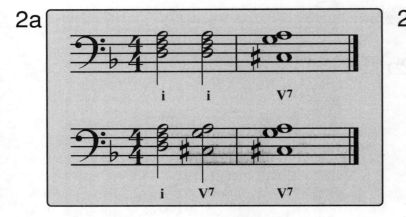

2b

2c
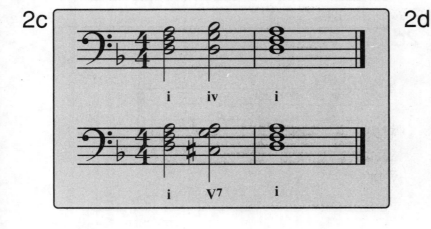

2d
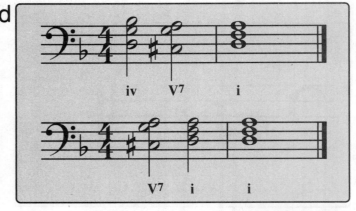

TEACHER: See page 47.

Primary Chords in D Minor

1. Your teacher will play melodies and chords in D minor.
   Write the Roman numeral names (**i**, **iv** or **V⁷**) on the lines below the staff.

2. Your teacher will play melodies that use notes from the D HARMONIC MINOR SCALE.
   Draw the missing notes in the third measure, using the correct rhythm.

TEACHER: See page 47.

Use with pages 42–43.

$\frac{3}{8}$ Time Signature

1. Your teacher will clap a rhythm pattern.
   Draw the missing notes in the second measure, using ♩. ♩ or ♪

2. Your teacher will clap a rhythm pattern.
   Circle the pattern that you hear.

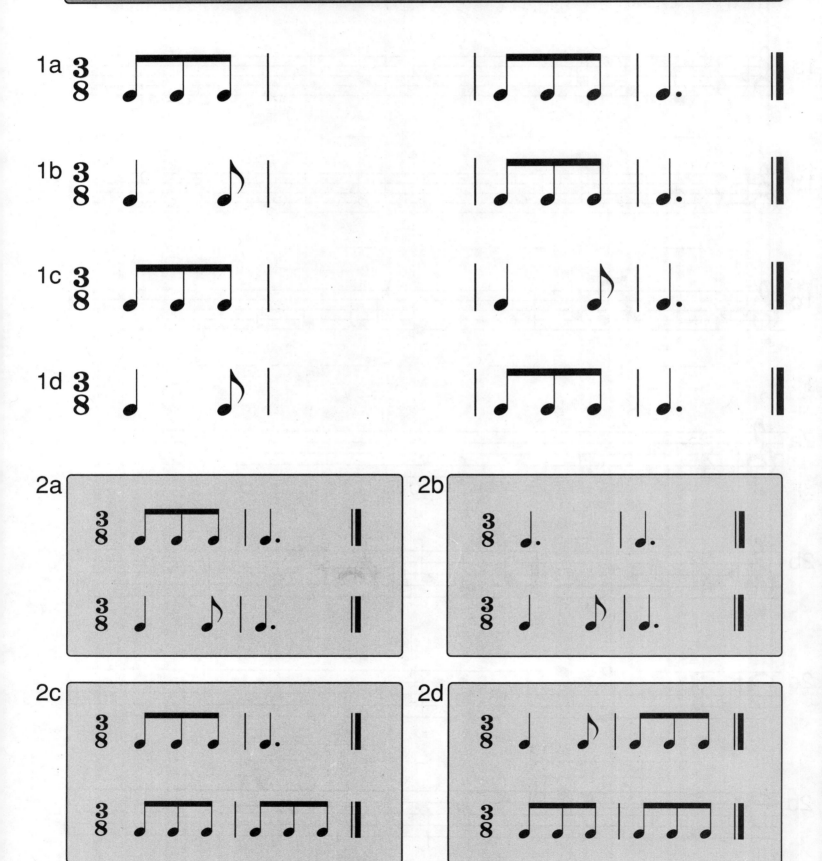

6/8 Time Signature

1. Your teacher will clap a rhythm pattern.
   Draw the missing notes in the second measure, using ♩. ♩. ♩ ♪♪♪ or ♪

2. Your teacher will play MELODIC intervals of a 4th, 5th or 6th ABOVE the given note.
   • Draw the second note on the staff, using a dotted quarter note.
   • Write the interval name (4, 5 or 6) on the line.

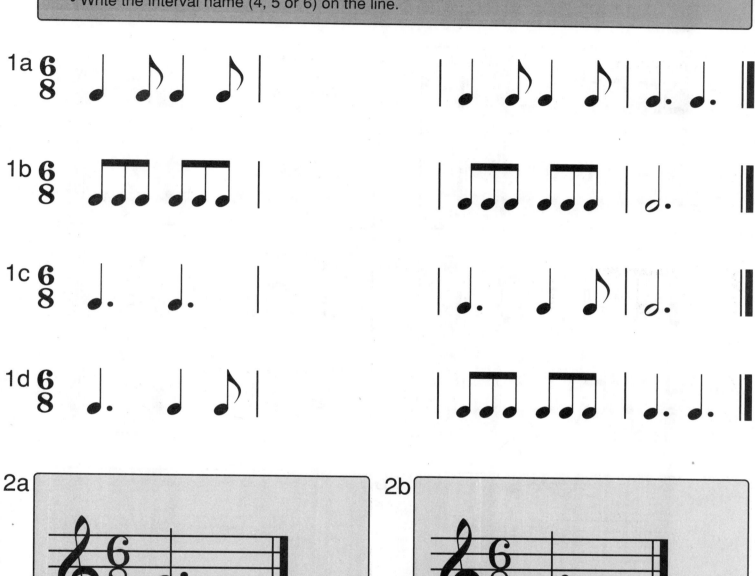

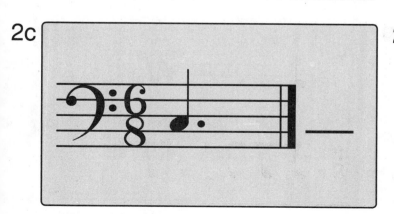

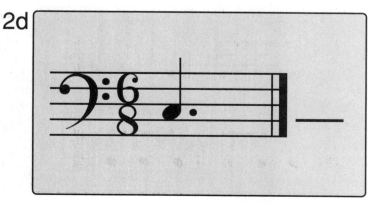

Use with pages 46–47.

$\frac{6}{8}$ Time Signature

1. Your teacher will clap a rhythm pattern.
   Circle the pattern that you hear.
2. Your teacher will play ALLEGRO and ANDANTE melodies.
   • Circle ALLEGRO if the melody is played QUICKLY, HAPPILY.
   • Circle ANDANTE if the melody is played MOVING ALONG.

1a

1b

1c

1d

2a

Allegro

ANDANTE

2b

Allegro

ANDANTE

2c

Allegro

ANDANTE

2d

Allegro

ANDANTE

Review

1. Your teacher will play a BLOCK chord followed by a BROKEN chord.
   Write the notes of the BROKEN chord in the order that they are played, using QUARTER NOTES.

2. Your teacher will play **i**, **iv** and **V⁷** chords in the key of D minor.
   Circle the chords that you hear.

3. Your teacher will play the A NATURAL MINOR SCALE or the A HARMONIC MINOR SCALE.
   If the scale is HARMONIC MINOR, draw a SHARP (♯) in front of the 7th tones.

4. Your teacher will play a MAJOR or MINOR triad.
   Circle the triad that you hear.

5. Your teacher will clap a rhythm pattern.
   Circle the pattern that you hear.

1

2
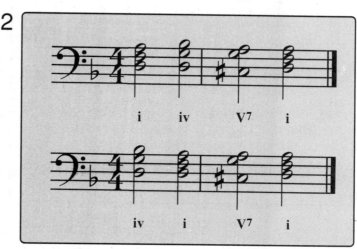

3

4
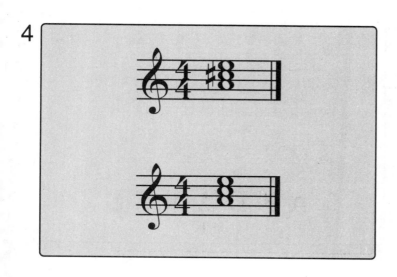

5

38

Teacher's Examples

Page 3 (Play)

Page 4 (Play)

Page 5 (Play)

Page 6 (Play)

Teacher's Examples

Page 7 (Play)

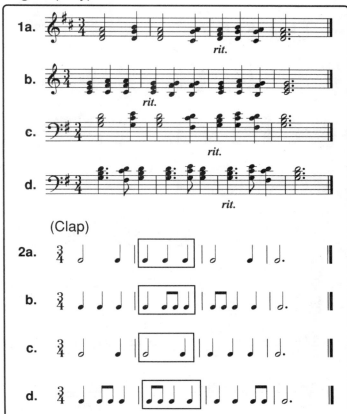

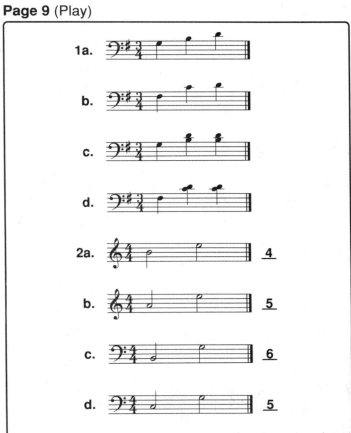

Page 9 (Play)

Page 8 (Play)

Teacher's Examples

Page 10 (Play)

Page 11 (Play)

Page 12 (Play)

Teacher's Examples

Page 13 (Play)

Page 14 (Play)

Page 15 (Play)

42

Teacher's Examples

Page 16 (Play)

Page 17 (Play)

Page 18 (Play)

Page 19 (Play)

Teacher's Examples

Page 20 (Play)

Page 21 (Play)

Page 22 (Play)

44

Teacher's Examples

Page 23 (Play)

Page 24 (Play)

Page 25 (Play)

(Clap)

Teacher's Examples

Page 26 (Play)

Page 27 (Play)

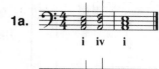

Page 28 (Play)

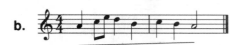

46

Teacher's Examples

Page 29 (Play)

Page 31 (Play)

Page 30 (Play)

47

Teacher's Examples

Page 32 (Play)

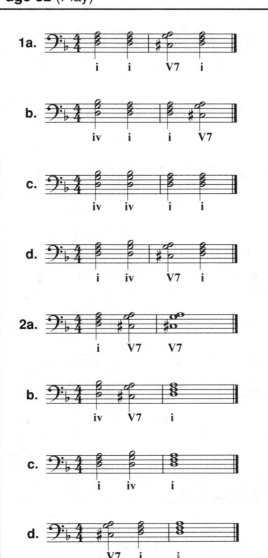

Page 33 (Play)

Page 34 (Clap)

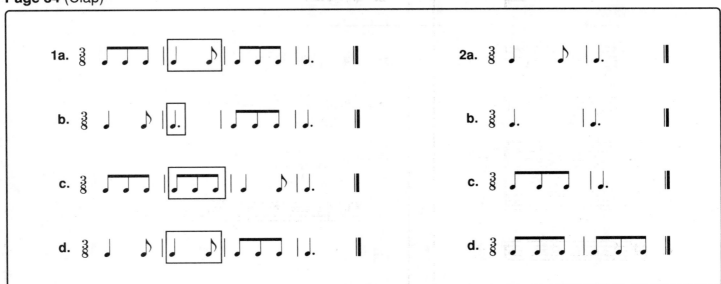

Teacher's Examples

Page 35 (Clap)

Page 36 (Clap)

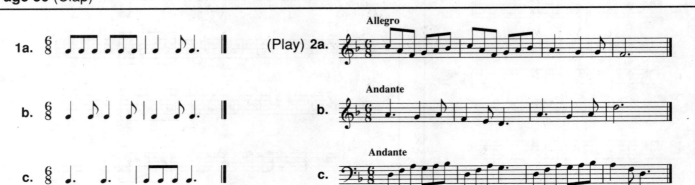

Page 37 (Play)